What Do You Do With a Tail Like This?

Steve Jenkins & Robin Page

Houghton Mifflin Harcourt Publishing Company, Boston 2009

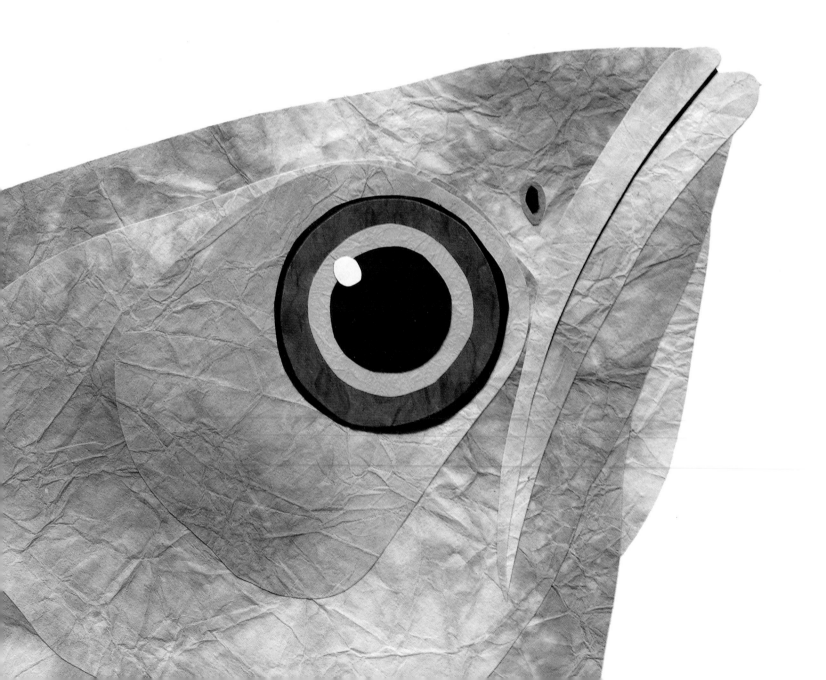

nimals use their noses, ears, tails, eyes, mouths, and feet in very different ways. See if you can guess which animal each part belongs to and how it is used. At the back of the book you can find out more about these animals.

What do you do with

a nose like this?

If you're a platypus, you use your nose to dig in the mud.

If you're a hyena, you find your next meal with your nose.

If you're an elephant, you use your nose to give yourself a bath.

If you're a mole, you use your nose to find your way underground.

If you're an alligator, you breathe through your nose while hiding in the water.

What do you do with
ears like these?

If you're a
jackrabbit,
you use
your ears
to keep
cool.

If you're a bat,
you "see" with your ears.

If you're a hippopotamus, you

If you're a cricket, you hear with ears that are on your knees.

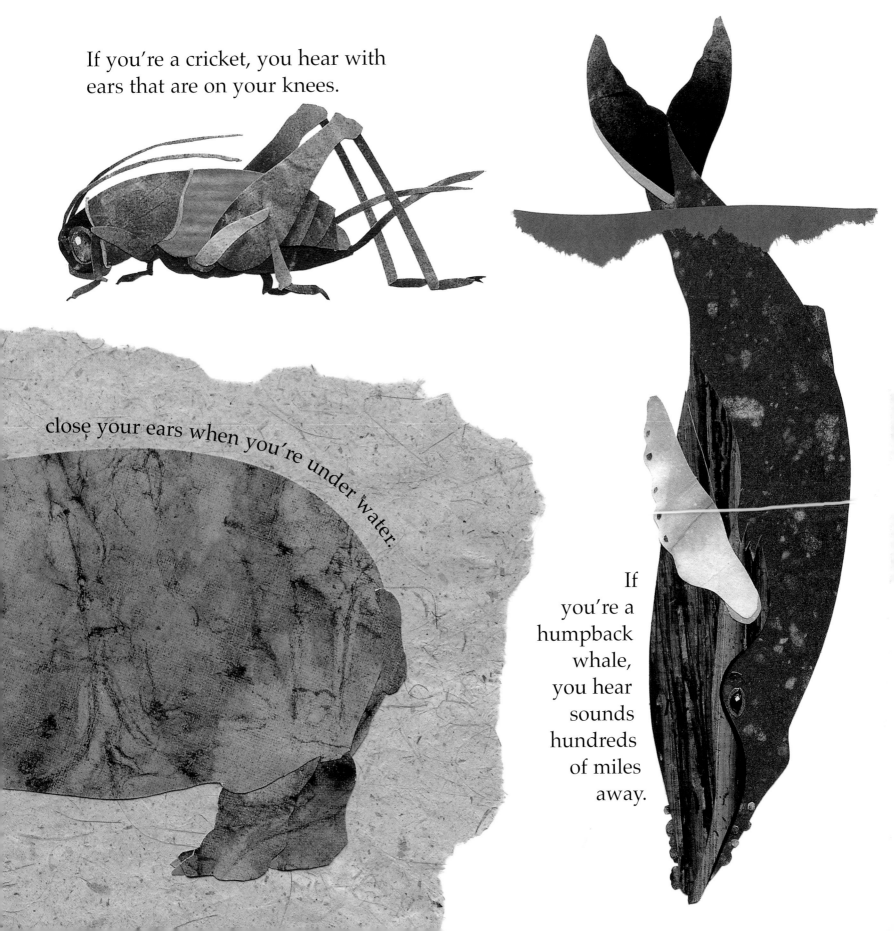

close your ears when you're under water.

If you're a humpback whale, you hear sounds hundreds of miles away.

What do you do with a tail like this?

If you're a giraffe, you brush off pesky flies with your tail.

If you're a skunk, you lift your tail to warn that a stinky spray is on the way.

If you're a lizard, you break off your

If you're
a monkey,
you
hang
from
a tree
by your
tail.

tail to get away.

If you're a scorpion,
your tail can give
a nasty sting.

What do you
do with eyes
like these?

If you're an eagle, you spot tiny animals from high in the air.

If you're a chameleon, you look two ways at once.

If you're a four-eyed fish, you look above and below the water at the same time.

If you're
a bush
baby,
you use
your
large eyes
to see
clearly
at night.

If you're a horned lizard, you squirt blood out of your eyes.

What do you do

with feet like these?

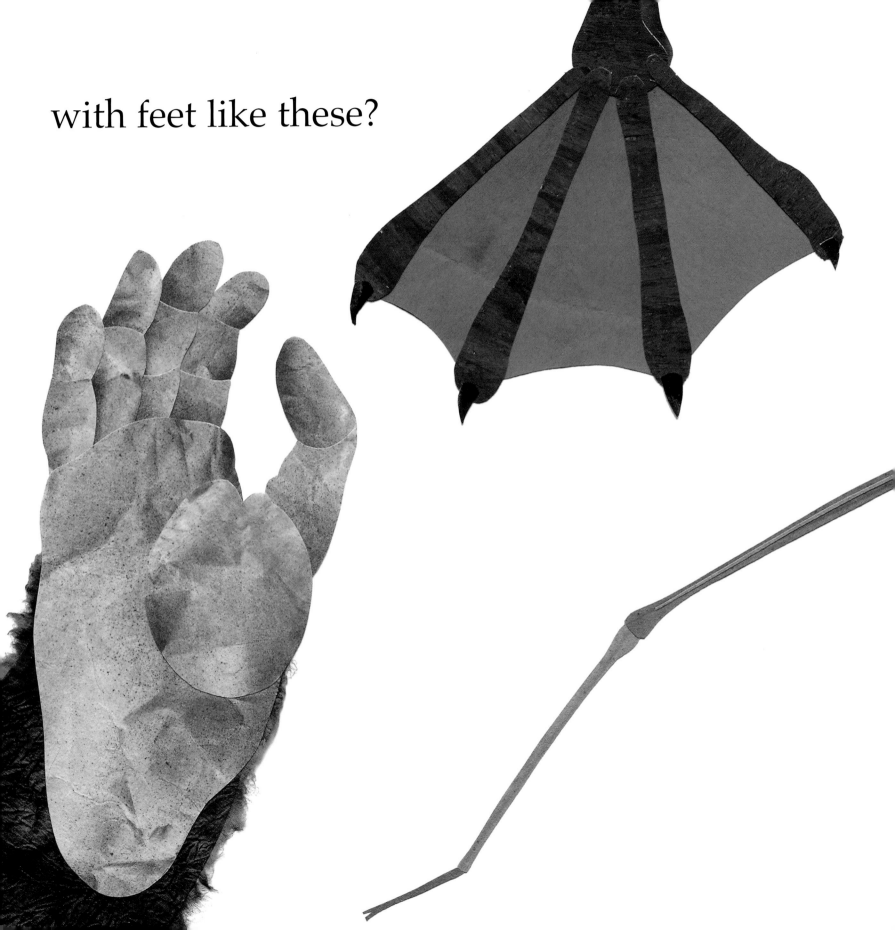

If you're
a blue-footed booby,
you do
a dance.

If you're a
chimpanzee,
you feed
yourself with
your feet.

If you're a water strider, you walk on water.

If you're a gecko, you use your sticky feet to walk on the ceiling.

If you're a mountain goat,
you leap from ledge to ledge.

What do you do with a mouth like this?

If you're a pelican, you use your mouth as a net to scoop up fish.

If you're an egg-eating snake, you use your mouth to swallow eggs larger than your head.

If you're a mosquito, you use your mouth to suck blood.

If you're
an archerfish,
you catch
insects by
shooting them
down with a
stream of water.

If you're an anteater, you capture termites with your long tongue.

NOSES

The **platypus**, a very unusual animal, lives in streams, ponds, and rivers in Australia. It's a mammal, but it lays eggs. Its feet are webbed, and the males have poisonous spurs on their back legs. Platypus poison probably wouldn't kill a person, but getting spurred is very painful and can be deadly for small animals. The platypus closes its eyes under water and uses its sensitive bill to detect the faint electric pulses emitted by its prey. Then with its bill it sifts though the mud for these small fishes, frogs, and insects. Platypuses are usually about 20 inches long and weigh about 5 pounds.

The **hyena**, found in Africa and parts of Asia, is usually thought of as a scavenger. Though hyenas are scavengers at times, they are also accomplished hunters, working in packs to pull down grazing animals that are much larger than themselves. Weighing up to 150 pounds, the hyena has an exceptionally keen nose and is able to detect prey at great distances.

The world's largest land animal, the **African elephant** can stand 13 feet tall and weigh more than 14,000 pounds. One of the elephant's most unusual features is its long nose, or trunk. With its trunk an elephant can breathe, pick things up, suck up and spray water, communicate with other elephants, bathe, and defend itself. The trunk alone may weigh 400 pounds and be more than 6 feet long. It has two thumblike projections on the end that allow the animal to grasp the leaves, grass, and fruit it likes to eat. The entire human body has more than 600 muscles, but there are as many as 100,000 muscles in an elephant's trunk.

The **American alligator** is found in swamps and rivers in the southeastern United States. Alligators grow to be 14 feet long and weigh as much as 1,000 pounds. They eat fish, turtles, birds, and other small animals. Alligators use their noses and tails to dig "gator holes," some as big as swimming pools, in the swamp. These holes don't dry up in times of drought, providing other animals with a source of water. Alligators hunt by lying quietly in the water, with only their eyes and noses sticking out. If an unlucky animal gets close enough, the alligator uses its powerful tail to lunge forward and grab it.

The **star-nosed mole** has twenty-two fleshy "fingers" on the end of its nose. This mole spends its whole life underground, where eyes are useless, so it uses its nose to find its way through a maze of tunnels. The mole eats worms, snails, and insects that it locates with the help of its sensitive nose, using both smell and touch. The star-nosed mole grows to 7 inches in length.

EARS

The **yellow-winged bat**, like all bats, makes a constant series of clicks or chirps as it flies. Most of these sounds are pitched too high for humans to hear. These sounds bounce, or echo, off nearby objects. By listening to the echoes, a bat can maneuver in the dark, avoid obstacles, and even find and catch the flying insects it eats. The yellow-winged bat lives in central Africa and has a wingspan of about 14 inches.

The **field cricket's** ears are on its two front legs. Openings in the cricket's hard outer covering lead to chambers inside each leg. By pointing its body (and its ears) in different directions, the cricket can tell where a sound is coming from. Field crickets, which are about ¾ inch long and live throughout North America, make their familiar chirping sound by rubbing the edges of their wings together. The warmer the temperature, the faster they chirp. Counting the number of chirps in 15 seconds and adding 40 gives a fairly accurate temperature reading (in degrees Fahrenheit).

The **antelope jackrabbit** is actually a hare, a close relative of rabbits. It has very long ears, up to a third its body length, and lives in the hot desert climate of the American Southwest. Its large ears help it stay cool by radiating excess body heat. The antelope jackrabbit eats grass and shrubs and can grow to 2 feet in length.

The **hippopotamus** is easily sunburned and spends much of its time under water. These large animals — 9 feet long and easily weighing 3,000 pounds — live in Africa and graze at night on grass and other plants around the lakes and rivers where they spend most of their time. Hippos close their ears and noses when they go under water, where they can stay as long as thirty minutes at a time.

The ears of the **humpback whale** are visible only as small openings in the whale's head. Whales need streamlined bodies that can move easily through the water, and external ears would slow them down. The humpback's hearing, however, is very sensitive. These whales communicate with one another by singing songs, and though we don't know exactly what the songs mean, we do know that whales can hear one another when they're hundreds of miles apart. These large mammals can be 50 feet long and weigh a ton per foot. They are filter feeders, eating millions of tiny plankton every day. Humpback whales are found in all of the world's oceans.

TAILS

The **striped skunk** is found throughout much of North America. Like other skunks it has the ability to spray attackers with a foul-smelling, eye-stinging liquid. Skunks are omnivores — they eat just about anything, including insects, fish, small mammals, bird eggs, fruit, and seeds. They can be longer than 2 feet and weigh as much as 14 pounds, though most are smaller. The striped skunk first warns an enemy to back off by raising its tail. If that doesn't

work, it stands on its front legs, arches its back, and shoots its spray over its head, so it never has to turn its back on an attacker. Skunk spray is effective up to ten feet away.

The world's tallest animal is the **giraffe**. It lives on the savannahs of Africa and can grow up to 19 feet in height. The giraffe feeds on leaves at the tops of the trees that dot these grasslands — leaves that other grazing animals can't reach. It protects itself against its primary enemy, the lion, with kicks from its powerful back legs and uses its long tail to brush flies and other insects from its back.

The **five-lined skink** has a long tail that can break off if it is attacked. The wriggling tail can distract predators, allowing the lizard to get away. This skink, which is 5 to 8 inches long, lives in the eastern part of the United States and eats insects and worms. Losing its tail doesn't really hurt the lizard — it soon grows a new one.

The **scorpion** is an ancient relative of the spider. Scorpion fossils older than 400 million years have been found, some of them 3 feet long. Today, scorpions grow to a maximum length of 8 ½ inches. They live in warm climates throughout the world and eat spiders, lizards, and small mammals. Hunting at night, scorpions locate their prey by touch and use the poison stinger at the end of their tail to paralyze an animal before it can get away.

The **spider monkey** can use its tail like a fifth "hand." The end of its tail has a patch of bare skin with a special groove that helps it grasp things. The spider monkey, along with the other monkeys living in Central and South America, is a New World monkey. New World monkeys are the only primates with a grasping, or prehensile, tail. The spider monkey's tail is longer than its body, which can be as tall as 2 feet. The spider monkey often hangs by its tail while eating fruit, leaves, and flowers.

EYES

The **chameleon** is found in Africa, Asia, and Europe. It hunts insects by sight, relying on its wide-set eyes to give it good depth perception. It also has to watch out for predators, and can swivel each of its eyes independently in any direction. The chameleon catches insects by quickly flicking out its sticky tongue, which is longer than its body. This tree-dwelling lizard grows up to 27 inches in length and has the unusual ability to change its skin color to match its surroundings.

The **bald eagle** lives throughout much of North America and is the national bird of the United States. It hunts by sight, soaring high in the air and looking for rabbits, small birds, and fish. Its eyesight is four to eight times as sharp as that of a human. The bald eagle is a large bird, with a wingspan of more than 7 feet. When it dives to attack prey, it can reach speeds faster than 150 miles per hour. The bald eagle is not really bald. Its head is covered with white feathers.

The **horned lizard**, often called a "horny toad," lives in the American Southwest. It is small, 3 to 5 inches in length, and covered with sharp spikes. This lizard feeds on ants and other insects and protects itself in an unusual way. If threatened, it first tries holding very still. If that doesn't work, it puffs itself up with air to make itself look larger. If it still feels threatened, it will squirt streams of blood from the corners of its eyes. This probably confuses an attacker, giving the horned lizard time to get away.

In the rivers of South America lives a fish that can look above and below the water at the same time. The **four-eyed fish** actually has just two eyes, but each eye is divided, with separate pupils, irises, and corneas. As it swims along the surface of the water, the top half of each eye can look up and watch for predators or insects to eat. The lower half, meanwhile, is looking down to find prey or watch for danger that might come from below. The four-eyed fish about 10 inches long.

British explorers in Africa heard sounds in the night that sounded like the cries of lost children. That's how the **bush baby**, a relative of the lemur and monkey, got its name. This tree-dwelling mammal is only 6 to 9 inches tall and weighs less than half a pound. It sleeps during the day and hunts insects, lizards, and mice at night. The bush baby has very large, round eyes that allow it to see in dim nighttime light. Its eyes don't move in their sockets, so the bush baby is constantly turning its head from side to side.

FEET

Chimpanzees are humans' closest animal relatives. These intelligent animals live in the forests of Africa and are typically 5 feet tall and 135 pounds. Like people, they have an opposable thumb. Unlike us, they also have an opposable big toe. This allows them to pick up and manipulate things with their feet. They eat fruit, leaves, insects, and the occasional small animal.

The male **blue-footed booby** uses its bright blue feet to attract a mate. Blue-footed boobies live on the tropical Pacific coasts of North and South America, where they catch the fish that make up their entire diet. They are large birds, with a wingspan of about 5 feet. When a male booby wants to impress a female, he does an elaborate dance, lifting his bright blue feet one at a time. At the same time, he points his beak to the sky, spreads his wings wide, and whistles.

The common **water strider**, found throughout the United States, lives on calm rivers and ponds. On the ends of its long legs it has tiny hairs that enable it to walk on top of the water. The water strider doesn't sink because of surface tension (the same effect causes water to bead up on a waxed surface, like a car). The water strider, with a body less than an inch long, skates along on top of the water and eats dead insects that it finds floating there.

If you've spent time in the tropics, you've probably seen small lizards walking on the walls or ceiling. These noisy, insect-eating reptiles are **geckos**. Their name probably comes from the unusual chirping sound they make. The bottom of the gecko's feet are covered with millions of tiny hairs and pads that use an electrical charge to cling to just about any surface — even a sheet of glass. Most geckos are about 7 inches long.

The **mountain goat**, found in the mountains of northwest North America, is not really a goat — it's more closely related to antelopes. This animal is at home on very steep, rocky slopes, where it is safe from most predators. The mountain goat has special hooves that allow it to travel where other animals can't. These hooves combine a hard outer covering, used for gripping small rock ledges, with a soft, nonskid pad. The mountain goat, which may be 4½ feet tall and weigh as much as 300 pounds, can move lightly and easily over almost sheer cliff faces. Avalanches and rockslides are dangerous, however: they kill more mountain goats than predators do.

MOUTHS

The **brown pelican**, found along the coasts of North and South America, has a large pouch of skin on the bottom part of its bill. The pelican flies sixty or seventy feet above the water, looking for fish. When it spots a school, it dives into the water and opens its mouth. Its pouch expands into a kind of net and can hold as much as three gallons of water and fish. The pelican then strains off the water and eats the fish. Brown pelicans are large birds, up to 4½ feet long.

The tiny **mosquito** is the animal that is most dangerous to humans. That's because in some parts of the world this insect can spread deadly diseases as it sucks blood. The mosquito has a special needlelike nose that it uses to pierce the skin of a person or animal. As it sucks blood through a hollow tube, it injects chemicals into the skin that keep the blood from clotting. These chemicals are what cause the uncomfortable itching we feel when bitten by a mosquito.

The **giant anteater** lives in Central and South America. Most of its diet consists of termites, rather than ants, and it can eat up to 30,000 of these a day. The giant anteater can be 8 feet long and weigh 100 pounds. It has an elongated, tubular mouth with no teeth and a tongue that is 2 feet long. It uses this sticky tongue to capture insects.

The **egg-eating snake** has jaws that can unhinge and very elastic skin, which allow it to eat eggs that are wider than its own body. It sometimes takes the snake several hours to swallow an egg. It has no teeth but breaks the egg with a special bone in its throat. This African snake eats as many eggs as it can during the birds' breeding season, then goes without food for the rest of the year. It grows to about 2½ feet in length.

The **archerfish** hunts by looking for insects on branches hanging low over the water. It has large eyes set well forward on its head, which give it good depth perception. When it spots a butterfly, beetle, or other insect, the archerfish squirts water out of its mouth and knocks the insect into the water, where it can be eaten. This small fish, about 10 inches long, can shoot a stream of water as far as three feet. Archerfish live in quiet waters from the east coast of Africa to Australia.

For Jamie, Alec, and Page

Copyright © 2003 by Steve Jenkins and Robin Page

All rights reserved. For information about permission to
reproduce selections from this book, write to:
Permissions
Houghton Mifflin Harcourt Publishing Company
215 Park Avenue South
New York, NY 10003

www.hmhbooks.com

The text of this book is set in Palatino.
The illustrations are cut-paper collage.

Library of Congress Cataloging-in-Publication Data is on file.

This edition published specially for Kohl's © 2009
by Steve Jenkins and Robin Page

ISBN: 978-0-547-25555-2

Printed in Singapore